Women In Culture
Past, Present, And Future

Women In Culture
Past, Present, And Future

Find Yourself

Ismay V. Harvey

To order additional copies of this book, contact:
Xlibris Corporation
1-888-795-4274
www.Xlibris.com
Orders@Xlibris.com
45450

Contents

Dedication

To all women leaders, both past and present, our future generation needs you.

To my spiritual father, mentor, and pastor, A. R. Bernard, whose visionary leadership inspired my own with what he has accomplished.

To my first lady Elder Karen Bernard, thank you for your spiritual discernment to me and all our CCC sisters.

To my sisters in the CCC wardrobe ministry, I have learned so much from them, and they laughed with me even when they did not know what I was going through.

To my cash flow group, when we meet for game night they do not want to go home.

To my telephone prayer partners, thank you for your dedication, perseverance, consistency, and also your support and prayers. We pressed on even when our flesh would get in the way and tell us we did not have to pray.

To all women young and old in the United States and other countries. I hope and pray that you gain something positive from reading these pages.

To the source of our lives and the source of our supply, we say thank you.

Acknowledgments

Writing this book was a bigger project than I anticipated since it was my first time writing a book and I had no idea what I was doing. What I did know was that I started and I had to finish.

It took a long time for me to find out that what I should of done last I did first. But thank God for the few dedicated individuals who came alongside and helped me in whatever way they could. We don't achieve anything in life without the help of individuals who have contributed to our lives. We are all the sum total of what we have learned from others.

To my sons Nigel and Justin, they did not take me seriously at first but now give me their support. Thank you.

To Nigel and Carmen and my granddaughters Britney, Jasmine, and Nya. To my sisters Elaine, Nola, Bernice, Stella, and Cynthia, and all my nieces and nephews and their children and extended families. Thank you.

To all my friends, some of whom I attended elementary and high school and remained friends with through the years, even when we did not agree on certain things. Thank you.

To our youth, our young leaders of the next generation. I appreciate the contribution you bring to the world, you are leaders in your own way. I want you to know that we have learned and are still learning from what you have to offer. Thank you.

Introduction

In August of 2004, I took a cruise with the Pointers. This was my first cruise and we went to Puerto Rico, St. Thomas, and a few other islands. I had a wonderful time. At each island we stopped at, we went on inner country trips where we learned a lot about the island's cultures and how the inhabitants operate and make a living.

On one island, we were taken in small boats to go from one island to another. This is how they did their shopping on a daily basis. On another one of our trips, we went to the beach. Oh what a wonderful day we had, the water was so blue and clean; even though it poured rain that day, it did not stop us. We stayed in the water all day; it was so relaxing. I will never forget that trip to the beach. In the evening, we would go back to our ship, relax for awhile, and then let go. Some of us went dancing, others went to different shows, while others just wanted to sit around with their friends and have a quiet evening.

After having such a wonderful time on that cruise, I decided to take another Carnival cruise the next year. I now had a passion for learning about the cultures of other countries and islands. These two trips encouraged me to write this book.

The ideas on these pages should teach us that there can be both sadness and happiness in learning about other cultures. I believe that my life story is being written one day at a time, and with God's help, it can and will be a masterpiece to help the next generation.

Ruth, Naomi, and I, Women of Different Cultures

Elimelech, Naomi's husband, had moved his family from one town to another because of a famine in the land. Sometimes in life we move due to certain circumstances and situations we are facing at the time, not knowing that these circumstances can be temporary. But most times it takes a crisis in our lives to find out; Naomi's family learned the hard way. The move they made was not the will of God.

There are times when we hear inside voices, or people tell us to do certain things which might seem right, but we have to ask ourselves, is it right for us? In life we make mistakes, but God has a way of using the things he didn't plan to work in our favor.

The Story of Ruth—What the Story Is About

Ruth was poor, a foreigner, and a woman and all this counted against her, but she was helped by Naomi, an older woman, to overcome the difficulties she faced. She had the good sense to listen to the advice given to her by Naomi, and Naomi was rewarded with Ruth's unfaltering loyalty. Ruth's story illustrates the triumph of courage and ingenuity over adverse circumstances. Four women are included in the genealogy and Ruth is one of the four.

The story contains four different episodes that together form a beautifully constructed novella:

1. *Naomi and Ruth go to Bethlehem* (Ruth 1)—The anguish of loss. Naomi and her family suffered great misfortune in a foreign land. Naomi returned to her home, Bethlehem, with her foreign daughter-in-law Ruth, in time for the barley harvest.

2. *Ruth meets Boaz* (Ruth 2)—The love story. Ruth, a young widow, met Naomi's relative, a rich man named Boaz. It seemed to have been love at first sight for him and he ordered that Ruth be well treated when she worked in his fields. Naomi saw immediately what was happening and encouraged Ruth to continue working in Boaz's fields.

3. *Ruth proposes marriage to Boaz* (Ruth 3)—This chapter contains some ribald peasant humor. Ruth approached Boaz during the night, on the threshing floor, and the text obliquely suggests that there may have been some sexual hanky-panky. Subsequently, Ruth suggested that they marry, reminding Boaz of his obligation to her as her nearest male kin. Boaz promised to do all he could.

4. *Ruth and Boaz marry* (Ruth 4)—The happy ending. Boaz proved as good as his word, and he and Ruth were married. She had a son named Obed, who would grow up to be the grandfather of King David, and Naomi cared for the child.

Naomi and Ruth Go to Bethlehem (Book of Ruth, Chapter 1)

Naomi was an Israelite woman who, during a famine, had gone with her family to live in the country of Moab. When her husband and two sons died, she decided to return to her hometown of Bethlehem. She had two daughters-in-law, Ruth and Orpah. All three women were widows. In modern society, a widow is free to remarry after her husband dies, but in ancient Israel this was not necessarily so. After her husband's death, a widow was still considered to be a part of her dead husband's family, because marriage joined families as well as individuals.

Her two daughters-in-law, Ruth and Orpah, were Moabite women, not Israelites. The Moabite people were traditional enemies of the Israelites. There was frequent warfare between the two groups. Naomi assumed that Ruth and Orpah would not want to return to Bethlehem with her even though the women respected and loved each other.

Orpah decided to return to her people and the Moabite way of life, but Ruth could not be persuaded. She had shared loneliness, anxiety, and grief with Naomi and now that the older woman was completely alone, Ruth would stand by her and go to Bethlehem. So the two women traveled to Bethlehem in time for the autumn harvest of barley.

Ruth Meets Boaz (Chapter 2)

Now although Naomi was destitute, she had good family connections. Furthermore, both she and Ruth were women of initiative. They did not believe in sitting down and letting events simply happen. Ruth decided she would help to glean the barley in the fields, to feed herself and Naomi and to get a store of grain for the winter. Gleaning was a common practice in ancient Israel. It was a form of charity for the disadvantaged in society (see Leviticus 23:22 and Deuteronomy 24:19). Recognized groups of the poor, such as widows, orphans, and foreigners, could walk behind the harvesters, picking up what was left. This is what Ruth did.

Ruth 2:3 says that "as it happened" Ruth went to the field of Naomi's rich relative Boaz. This phrase is often used in the Bible to suggest that something significant is about to happen. It also implied, with a touch of Jewish humor, that Naomi saw a good match for Ruth and coaxed her into meeting Boaz.

Naomi knew that Ruth was beautiful and respected, and she knew that a rich husband for Ruth would solve all their problems. Boaz was the ideal choice. He was available, childless, well respected, and rich. He was also a relative of Naomi's through her husband's family, so he had a legal obligation to help Naomi. Boaz was second in line as the closest relative in Naomi's, and therefore Ruth's, family.

A *go'el* was a close male relative with the duty of looking after a family when the male head of the family was absent. In earlier times, the family was expected to marry the widow of an Israelite man if she wished it. Ruth, who may not have understood the niceties of Israelite law, called Boaz *go'el*. By great good luck, Boaz seemed to have been smitten from the outset. He went to great lengths to get extra grain for Ruth, to protect her from young men who might harass her, and to see that she was properly fed.

Of course, the point of the story is that it was not just love or luck, but God who was nudging them into their destiny.

Ruth Proposes Marriage to Boaz (Chapter 3)

This part of the story took place on the threshing floor, at a golden time of the year when the harvest had been brought in and the weather was still warm. Love was in the air, with the fertility of nature reflected in the lives of the characters.

Naomi devised a plan to prod Boaz into proposing to Ruth. She knew men, and she gave Ruth specific instructions on everything she must do.

Fortunately, Ruth had the good sense to heed the older woman. She perfumed herself, dressed in her most becoming clothes, and waited until Boaz had eaten a good meal—both women knew a man with a full stomach was easier to handle. When Boaz finally laid down to sleep, Ruth approached him on the threshing floor—someone always slept there at night until the grain was removed, to guard against thieves.

This action would seem strange unless you knew that in ancient times "foot" was a euphemism for the male genital organ, as "sandal" was used for the female organ. At harvest time, threshing floors at harvest time were often the scene of sexual shenanigans, what the old Irish priests used to rail against as "frolicking in the fields," a time for license of which was forbidden at other times.

Lying beside Boaz, Ruth suggested that he, as the *go'el* of Naomi's family, should "cover her with his blanket," a euphemism for marriage. She had the right to demand marriage of the *go'el* of her family so she could have the children that Israelite women longed for. Boaz happily agreed, but pointed out that there was another man who had that right, a closer relative even than himself. Boaz had to square matters with him before he could marry Ruth. He seemed to have been at pains to do everything correctly so that there could be no question about the legality of the marriage.

Ruth stayed beside Boaz until morning, stealing away before the first light to return to Naomi, who pounced on her and demanded to know how things had gone and whether the plan had worked. Was Ruth to be married or single? The two women waited impatiently to see how events would unfold.

The Marriage of Ruth and Boaz (Chapter 4)

Of course, the villagers were well aware of what was happening, as people in small towns usually are. When Boaz went the next morning to the meeting place at the gate of the town, he was met almost immediately by the official *go'el* of Naomi's family—and probably by a good many intrigued onlookers as well.

Some complicated negotiations went on regarding a small parcel of land that Naomi either owned outright or had put up for sale at some previous time, but this was just a formality. The outcome of this story was never in doubt.

So Boaz took Ruth and she became his wife. When they came together, the Lord made her conceive, and she bore a son. Then the women said to Naomi, "Blessed be the Lord, who has not left you this day without next of kin. May his name be renowned in Israel! He shall be to you a restorer of life and nourishment for your old age. For your daughter-in-law who loves you, who is more to you than seven sons, has borne him." Reference? Then Naomi took the child and laid him on her bosom and became his nurse.

Ruth and Boaz were married and she had a son, Obed. Eventually, Ruth would be the great-grandmother of King David. The marriage of Ruth and Boaz created a family with a good chance of success because:

- Naomi was shrewd, courageous, and persevering.
- Ruth was intelligent, strong, loyal, and level-headed.
- Boaz was a good manager of people, and not afraid to get his hands dirty.

How the Story of Ruth and Naomi Relates to My Life

My name is Ismay Walker Harvey I am the last child of seven siblings. I was born in Trinidad, West Indies. My mom died when I was eight years old. I grew up with my grandmother who raised my younger brother and me. We never knew our father and the only memory I have of my mother is of her selling candy at the elementary school I attended and her coming to see my brother and me when she could. My second oldest brother also lived with us and was able to help out financially because my family was very poor. When I was fourteen, my grandmother became ill and I had to take care of her. This was a difficult task for me seeing as I was only in high school. My Aunt Mel and her husband, who were traveling evangelists with the Salvation Army, had to relocate back to Trinidad to be near her mother, which was of great help to me. They did not live with us but lived close by.

My grandmother died when I was fifteen years old, and I had to move in with my Aunt Mel and her husband, which was a completely different lifestyle for me seeing that my aunt and uncle were Christians. I started attending church with them, which I loved. After I graduated from high school, my aunt and uncle were sent to another country in North America and I was not allowed to go with them, so other provisions were made. They arranged for me to stay in one of the Salvation Army's Girls hostels and my older brothers and sisters helped out financially until I could find a job, which was difficult. I found work in factories. At that time I also dated my first boyfriend and became pregnant. I had to have an abortion since children were not allowed in the girls hostel. I had to move out and stay with one of my sisters, her children, and my great-aunt, which made for an overcrowded situation. However, what was important was that I had a roof over my head and food on the table and was able to help my sister in the area of babysitting. It was around that time that I realized I had to do something with my life. I also realized that I had a gift that I could not quite explain: it had to do with the power of healing and helping others.

One day, I received a letter from my aunt in South America stating that my Uncle Will was very ill with a strange disease. I read the letter and was staring out the window when the thought came to mind that if I was there, I could help him. I could not explain how, just that I could. I kept praying for him and knew in my heart that he would be alright. A few weeks later I received another letter from my aunt stating that my uncle was doing much better. I believe this gift is due to an accident I had at the age of seven. I lived in a three-story building with terraces. I was playing with my friends on the second-floor terrace while my brother was downstairs playing with his friends. A fight erupted and my brother decided to run upstairs. One of his friends grabbed a rock and threw it upstairs with the intention of hitting him on his way up. Instead, I was hit in the head with the rock and had to be taken to the emergency room. When I arrived at the hospital, I immediately went into a coma. I remained in a coma for a few weeks and no one thought I would make it, but God had a plan and a purpose for my life. I strongly believe that this is when my gift started to unfold. Something happened when I was in the coma that changed my life. The only way I can explain this change is that I am a spirit being living in two worlds. I have a strong relationship with my maker, God the father, Jesus Christ his son, and the Holy Spirit, my mentor, we communicate dreams, revelations, and visions. I can see and hear things that others may not be able to see or hear. The Holy Spirit reveals things to me and I believe that I am here on this earth for a purpose. I get frustrated at times when I cannot explain my purpose to others.

I migrated to the United States in October 1966. My first job was with the N.Y. Telephone Co. I attended night school where I received my GED and a few college credits. My next jobs were at the Public Library, the bank, and, finally, with the City of New York Department of Social Services as a caseworker, where I worked for twenty-five years (1976-2001) before retiring. The job was very interesting. I was able to help with the needs of individuals and families. I enjoyed working with the public, especially with single mothers with young children. Because of my experiences raising my son as a single mother, I was able to relate to their situations. The job also taught me what it was like to be on both sides of the fence. One year before working with the city of New York, I received public assistance/welfare, but by the grace of God, I was able to get my act together. I passed the New York City test, and was called for a position in the same building where I received welfare, so I knew off-hand what the clients were going through and how to communicate with them. It is so important to treat others the way we would like to be treated.

In 1994, my son, at the age of 19 years old, was shot and almost lost his life. If it wasn't for God's grace and mercy, he would not be alive today. He was hospitalized for almost a week, and after being discharged, he was immediately arrested. What started off as a snowball fight ended up with him being shot and arrested. He was able to make bail that day and he and his friends were offered probation. His friends took the deal, but he went to trial to explain his part in what happened. He lost the case and was sentenced to 42 months in jail?.

From that moment, our lives were changed. I had no idea what God was doing. I later found out that he was trying to get my attention. I took it very hard since he is my only child and I used to call him my miracle baby, since I was told I would not get pregnant and I always wanted to have children. At the time, I did not know much about God, but I knew there was a God and he answers prayers. He told me so in Jeremiah 29: 11, 12. Looking back, I believe God will do whatever it takes to get our attention, even if it hurts. He knew that there was work for me to do in fulfilling his purpose. He did not only save my son's life, but he saved my life. Today, I can say I am a work in progress, and I have learned that every problem is a wisdom problem. It's all about being able to listen through the voice of God and being obedient to what he says.

Women in Culture

Women have played many roles in various societies throughout history, including wife, mother, farmer, laborer, business executive, teacher, and volunteer worker. Most women have combined two or more of these roles.

Some societies have given women honor, others have considered women less important than men. Today, women in many countries make at least some of the decisions about what they will do with their lives. In the United States, Canada, and most European nations, a woman can choose whether she wants a career, whether she wants to marry, and whether she wants to raise children. In many countries throughout the world, women are challenging society's traditional image of what a woman may choose to be.

Most societies have related their ideas about women to beliefs about their physical characteristics. Some of these beliefs have little or no scientific basis. But they have been accepted for so many years that few people question them.

Women's Roles

Ancient Societies—Most women married and began raising children soon after reaching puberty. They remained at home, received no formal education, and had little economic or social power. Exceptions included the women judges who are mention in the Bible, and the women of ancient Egypt and Sparta. Both Egyptian and Spartan women could own and inherit property. In addition, Egyptian women could work outside the home, and Spartan women could receive a formal education.

Ancient Rome—Roman women had more legal and social freedom than most women in Europe for the next several centuries. They were highly respected, managed household affairs, and moved freely through the city to attend public functions.

India—Women owned property and took part in public debates thousands of years before the birth of Christ. Beginning in 200 B.C., Hinduism developed laws that gave women an inferior status to men. Most Hindu parents arranged for their daughters to be married before reaching puberty, and taught them to always obey their husbands. Later, other religions, including Christianity, adopted practices that gave men a status superior to that of women.

Early Modern Societies—Religion remained an important factor in determining women's positions. As Christianity spread through Europe, women lost much of the freedom they had had under Roman law. The Roman Catholic Church followed Old Testament law and early German tradition regarding male domination.

Most women received no formal education. Noble women learned to sew, spin, weave, and direct household servants.

Islam, the religion of the Muslims, spread through the Middle East, Northern Africa, and part of Europe and Asia from the 700s to the 1200s. Like Christianity and Hinduism, Islam taught women to obey their husbands.

Muslim women began wearing veils over their faces. Muslim women did not have the right to own property and divorce their husbands.

Before the 1800s, most women worked only in and around the home. In England, a number of women worked in trade. The few women who did work outside the home did not have the right to spend their own wages. Few women had any voice in politics or economics except through their husbands. Most European countries forbid wives to own property or to enter a profession.

Industrialized Societies

A shortage of men resulted in large numbers of women beginning to work outside the home. English and American textile mills were among the first factories to employ women in the early 1800s.

At first, the labor shortage assured fairly good working conditions for women, although they worked long hours and earned less than men. Unmarried working women gained some independence from their families because they could spend their earnings or save for an education. But many single women lived under strict supervision in dormitories operated by their employers. Married women had no legal right to do as they wished with their own earnings.

Some of the first organized attempts to improve a woman's status took place in the United States. These actions occurred in the areas of educational, social, and political reform. As women gained more education and greater opportunities to work outside the home, they began to demand other rights as well.

Women's Roles Today

In the 1970s and 1980s, more women went to college and held a wider variety of jobs than ever before. Women in many countries could, if they wished, live independently and control their own earnings and property. Women could vote and run for public offices in almost all countries that held elections.

The United Nations had a commission on the status of women. Many nations have agreed to follow the commission's policies on divorce, education, property rights, suffrage, and other issues related to women's rights.

Women in Other Countries—Women are given a greater voice in political and social matters by changing laws and customs. In 1960, Sirimavo Bandaranaike of Sri Lanka became the first female prime minister in the world. Since then, several other women have held the highest political office in their country. They include Indira Gandi of India, Golda Meir of Israel, Isabel Peron of Argentina, Margaret Thatcher of Great Britian, Gro Harlem Brundtland of Norway, and Corazon Aquino of the Philippines.

Africa—More women are being educated than ever before. About 40 percent of Kenya's high school pupils are women and the numbers are rising in other African countries. Some women have occupied important government positions such as, supreme court judge in Ghana and chief minister in Congo.

In the 1960s, 1970s, and 1980s, many women left their villages and devoted their lives to child rearing and housework.

Western Europe—Women make up a large portion of the labor force, but few hold high paying jobs. Although almost half the women in Sweden work, they make up only about 20 percent of their country's lawyers and 23 percent of the country's physicians. In West Germany, women make up more than a third of the labor force, but they hold only a low percentage of the best jobs. In Great Britain, only about 12 percent of the working women hold managerial positions. As elsewhere, many women in Western Europe are demanding increased rights.

South America—Most women accept traditional roles of housekeeping and raising families. But many who live in major cities or have had some high school education seek jobs outside the home. Most Latin American nations recognize the principle of equal pay for equal work, and most have women's bureaus connected with their department of labor. These bureaus teach women about their rights as workers and provide technical training to help women get better jobs.

Soviet Union—Women and men receive equal pay for equal work. Men still hold most top government positions, but they also do almost all the housework and shopping. The government provides nurseries where working mothers can leave their preschool children.

Women make up about half the Soviet labor force—about 70 percent of the nation's physicians, almost half of its judges, and a third of its engineers and lawyers are women. Women also make up 70 percent of teachers and about 60 percent of the economists. About a third of the members of the Supreme Soviet, the nation's parliament, are women.

China—As in the Soviet Union and other communist countries, society considers women equal to men and expects them to work just as hard. Women drive trucks, work on street construction crews, and fly military planes. Most of the nation's teachers are women. Working mothers leave their children in childcare centers or with elderly relatives. Many Chinese women hold important positions on local government bodies.

Japan—A growing number of married women work outside the home. They make up about 40 percent of the nation's workforce, but most of this group work in family-owned businesses.

India—Women have equal legal rights, including the right to vote and the right to own property. Political parties encourage women to run for political office. During the 1970s and 1980s, increasing numbers of educated working women emerged in India. But most of them came from the top levels of Indian society. About 22 percent of all Indian women can read and write, compared with about 46 percent of men.

Arab Lands—Women in some areas of Bahrain, Kuwait, and Saudi Arabia see few men outside their immediate families. Some restaurants and hotels in these areas separate men and women.

For centuries, Arab custom required women to veil their faces. In 1920, Turkey banned the veil. Iran abolished it in 1935. However, in 1979, revolutionaries took control of Iran and set up a government based on traditional Islamic customs. Many Iranian women then returned to wearing a traditional ankle-length garment call a *chuddar*. Today, few women wear veils in Egypt, Iraq, Lebanon, and Syria. Saudi Arabian law still requires veils, but many women choose veils of thin fabrics that do not conceal the face. Women make up about a fourth of all students in Arab universities. A small but growing percentage of women work outside the home, especially in professions such as teaching.

Culture

Culture is a term used by social scientists for a people's whole way of life. In everyday conversations, the culture may refer to activities in such fields as art, literature, and music. But to social scientists, a people's culture consists of the ideas, objects, and way of doing things created by the group.

Culture includes beliefs, customs, inventions, language, technology, and traditions. A culture is any way of life, simple or complex. It consists of learned ways of acting, feeling, and thinking. It is a set of simple extensions of various parts of the body. Culture enables people to do things their muscles and senses alone would not allow them to do. The human body needs oxygen, and a certain range of temperatures to live. However, cultural devices have enabled human beings to overcome some of the limitations of their bodies, and stay alive in harsh environments. Early culture was a means to extend the ability to obtain food, seek protection, and raise offspring. The ancestors of modern human beings had an advantage in the struggle for survival because they developed primitive tools or other cultures. As a result, the ability to create culture grew from generation to generation.

Characteristics of Culture

In his book *Primitive Culture* (1871), Sir Edward Burnett Tylor defined culture as "the complex whole which includes knowledge, beliefs, art, morals, law, customs, and any other capabilities and habits acquired by man as a member of society." Tylor's definition includes three of the most important characteristics of culture: (1) culture is acquired by people, (2) a person acquires culture as a member of society, and (3) culture is a complex whole. Culture is acquired by people because it consists of learned patterns of behavior rather than the biologically determined ones that are sometimes called instinctive. Culture includes the ways that the members of a society relate to one another. Human beings could not deal with one another unless culture defined what to do and expect; most large groups have cultural traits that meet the group's needs and ensure its survival, such a set of traits can be called a culture. Business companies, villages, and other social groups have their own cultural traditions. Many occupational groups, such as physicians, and ethnic groups, such as Chinese Americans and Mexican Americans, have their subcultures and also share the American culture.

Cultures That Resemble One Another

All cultures have features that result from basic needs shared by all people. Every culture has methods of obtaining food and shelter. It distributes the food and other goods to its people. Every culture has ways to protect itself against invaders. A culture has religious beliefs and a set of practices to express them. In addition, each culture has some type of scientific knowledge.

Cultures That Differ From One Another

Cultures differ from one part of the world to another, for example, eating, what people eat, how they eat, and how food is prepared differ from culture to culture.

Environmental differences, such as climate, land forms, mineral resources, native plants, and animals all influence culture. For example, most people in tropical regions wear draped clothing, which consists of one or more long pieces of cloth wrapped around the body. People in colder parts of the world wear tailored clothing, which is cut and sewn to fit the body. Tailored clothing provides more warmth than draped clothing. People do not realize how greatly culture influences their behavior until they come across other ways of doing things. Only then can they see that they have been doing things in a cultural way rather than in a natural way. For example, many westerners believe it is natural to look directly into a person's eye while talking, while others, such as people in some Asian nations, think it is rude to do so.

People are most comfortable within their own culture, and they prefer the company of others who share their culture. When people have to deal with others of another culture even small differences in behavior may make them uneasy. There is difficulty and uneasiness that people undergo when they leave their own culture and enter another. This is called *culture shock.*

Contact With Other Cultures

Contact between two societies with difference cultures causes change in both societies, they borrow cultural traits from each other, particularly if a newly learned trait seems better than a traditional one.

Diffusion is one of the most common causes of cultural change. Christianity, which originated in the Middle East, spread throughout the world by means of diffusion. Prolonged contact between cultures brings acculturation, a process in which people of one culture adopt traits from another. In most cases of acculturation, both cultures borrow from each other.

Assimilation takes place when immigrants or newcomers adopt the culture of the society in which they have settled. In some cases, assimilation leads to the disappearance of a minority group. The minority group disappears because its members lose the cultural characteristics that had set them apart.

Throughout history, many inventions have changed human culture.

Development in writing ranks as one of the most important steps in the growth of human culture. The first system of writing was developed about 350 B.C. in what is now southeastern Iraq. Others developed in China at about the same time. Writing enabled people to record their thoughts and discoveries for later use and to communicate over long distances. They also began to record aspects of their culture and hand it down in written form from generation to generation.

How Culture Changes

Some social scientists believe that many social problems come about because some parts of a culture change more slowly than others. Cultural lag refers to this tendency of certain parts of a culture to fall behind other related parts.

In the United States history, much cultural lag has occurred in customs, ideas, and other non-material parts of the national culture. Science and technology change so rapidly that they sometimes have outrun non-material culture.

In other societies and other times, changes in ideas have come before changes in the material culture; for example, physicians had the knowledge to perform some operations for thousands of years, but little surgery was possible until the discovery of antiseptics and painkillers in the 1800s.

A number of factors may cause a culture to change: (1) changes in the environment, (2) contact with other cultures, (3) invention, and (4) further development of the culture itself.

Cultural Change Today

The rate of cultural change has increased rapidly since the mid-1800s. This increase has occurred largely because of many advances in science and technology. Exchanges between cultures also have become more rapid and widespread since the mid-1800s. Because of airplanes, motion pictures, radio, and television, most of the cultural traditions in the world are continually in touch with one another.

Widespread cultural exchange seems to be producing a common world culture. As a result, many differences among people are disappearing. Some fear that this trend toward a common culture will deprive human beings of a variety of interesting ways of life. Others believe that the development of a world culture makes more variety available to each individual.

Culture of Animals

Scientists once thought that only human beings had culture, but most of them now believe that animals also have some elements of culture. The members of many species communicate with one another by means of signs. Many animals use various kinds of signs to communicate. Scientists have taught chimpanzees to "speak" to people in sign language. However, most scientists agree that any culture must include the use of symbols to be considered a true culture.

Understanding the Power of Culture

Every culture is built on a foundation of beliefs that shapes the culture. The culture shapes the people, and the people shape their lives. The influence of culture will affect factors such as the way we think, communicate, and raise our children; how our children view their parents; how we solve problems; sense of humor; standards of beauty; how we view others; laws; policies; values; and diet. One of the most nonviolent, most effective ways to destroy a nation of people is first to destroy its culture by attacking or eliminating the belief system on which the culture was built. When we lost our culture we lost our identity, and by losing our identity, we lost our sense of direction which eventually could lead to destruction.

Power of Culture

Because Israel's culture and beliefs were so intimately tied to their relationship with God, its cultural preservation was of the utmost importance. However, cultural preservation would not be an easy task. God knew if the Israelites lost their culture they would also lose their identity. If they lost their identity, they would lose their sense of direction, and if they lost their sense of direction, their people would eventually be destroyed.

Destruction of Culture

In the September 23, 1991 issue of *Time* magazine, the cover story, "Lost Tribes, Lost Knowledge," suggested that when native cultures disappear, so do scientific and medical wisdom. The slave owners did not respect the ideas, wisdom, or the cultural ways of their slaves, which were considered to be inferior to those of western culture.

Knowledge disappears when natives are stripped of their lands. Knowledge also disappears when the young who are in contact with the outside world embrace the view that traditional ways are illegitimate and irrelevant. Most cultures are destroyed because their ways and ideas are considered to be irrelevant by the stronger more powerful culture. Such was the case of the African slave; his language values, traditions, and beliefs were considered to be primitive.

Preserving Cultures

Never forget your history. You must teach it to your children and talk about it when you are at home or out for a walk, at bedtime and first thing in the morning. Cultures are preserved and maintained in the hearts and minds of young people. In our society, it is very difficult to maintain and preserve our own culture while living in a multicultural society because we have not been trained to respect, appreciate, and understand cultures that are different from our own. This is particularly true with the black culture. Since the time of slavery, the black culture has been discounted and classified as inferior and unimportant. Such standards dictate what should or should not be placed in textbooks, they determine what behavior is ethical or unethical, they define physical beauty.

Speaking the Language

Sometimes it is difficult to live with a culture we do not understand or find it difficult to communicate with. Communication is a key factor in living peacefully with other cultures. If we can't understand them, how will we know how to treat them or please them?

People are impressed when people of another culture can understand and communicate with a culture other than their own.

Respect for Different Cultures

No one has a right to discount or disrespect another man's cultural traditions and beliefs, if those beliefs and practices, however strange, do not violate God's law.

Women's Suffrage

Is it the right of women to vote? Today women in nearly all countries have the same voting rights as men. They did not begin to gain such rights until the early 1900s and they had to overcome strong opposition. The people who supported the drive for women's suffrage were call suffragists.

Changing social conditions for women in the early 1800s, combined with the idea of equality, led to the birth of the women's suffrage movement. For example, women began to receive more education and to take part in reform movements, which involved them in politics, which resulted in the right to vote.

Suffrage quickly became the chief goal of the women's rights movement. Leaders of the movement believed that if women had the vote, they could use it to gain other rights. The suffragists faced strong opposition. Opponents believed women were less intelligent and less able to make political decisions than men.

In Other Countries

In 1893, New Zealand became the first nation to grant women full voting rights. In 1902, Australia gave women the right to vote in national elections. In the 1900s, other countries enacted women's suffrage such as Finland, Germany, Great Britain, and Sweden. In the mid-1900s, China, France, India, Italy, Japan, and other nations gave women the vote. By the mid-1980s, only seven nations, all of them in the Middle East, still denied women the right to vote. They were Bahrain, Kuwait, Oman, Qatar, Saudi Arabia, the United Arab Emirates, and Yemen.—(Sana) "Anne Firor Scott" what is this?

Some Women's Organizations

The Women's Christian Temperance Union (WCTU) is an international organization of women who believe in personal and total abstinence from all alcoholic beverages and who work for the abolition of the liquor traffic. The program includes scientific narcotics education, good citizenship, child welfare, and world peace.

The WCTU has played an active part in getting laws passed which provide that young people in the public schools be taught the scientific facts about what alcohol is and what it does. The organization was founded in 1874. It has branches in all the states of the union as well as in Puerto Rico and the Virgin Islands. The organization grew out of the Women's Temperance Crusade in 1873.

The Temperance Crusade swept over 23 states, and resulted in the closing of thousands of places that sold liquor throughout the nation.

The organization grew rapidly, and influence increased with its growth.

The WCTU has national headquarters at 1730 Chicago Avenue, Evanston, IL 60211.

Women's Relief Corps National is the oldest women's patriotic organization in the United States. In July 1883, it was voted the official auxiliary of the Grand Army of the Republic.

The Women's Relief Corps is the only existing patriotic organization that was founded solely on the basis of loyal womanhood, regardless of kinship. They are located at 629 South Seventh Street, Springfield, IL 62703. The Women's Relief Corps' aims are to aid and memorialize the Grand Army of the Republic and perpetuate the memory of its dead. The organization also works to assist veterans of all U.S. wars. Members promote patriotism and take part in child welfare wars advocacy?.

Women's American ORT has about 145,000 members in the United States. It is a nonprofit agency founded in 1880 to save underprivileged and uprooted Jewish people from dependence upon charity by teaching them skills and trades.

The ORT program is financed by governments, local communities, the American Jewish Joint Distribution Committee and by affiliated groups. Headquarters are at 315 Park Avenue S., New York, NY 10010.

Women's Bureau is an agency of the United States Department of Labor. It develops policies and programs to improve the welfare and status of women in the workforce. The bureau is chiefly a fact-finding service, and promotional agency. It does not administer any laws. The Women's Bureau conducts research and develops programs to improve job opportunities for women and girls, especially in fields that have not traditionally been open to them. It encourages improved vocational counseling, better job-training programs, and continuing education for women. It works for the expansion of childcare and other supportive services. The bureau also promotes legislation to reduce sex discrimination in the workplace. It conducts or sponsors various studies and publishes findings. The Bureau provides information and assistance to individuals, employers, labor unions, schools, employment agencies, as well as federal, state, and local governments and international organizations. Congress established the Women's Bureau in 1920.

General Federation of Women's Clubs is an international organization of about 10 million women who belong to women's clubs in about 35 countries. The General Federation of Women's Clubs was founded in 1890. They are located at 1734 N. Street NW, Washington, DC 20036.

Samaria

The name "Samaria" derives from an ancient city of the same name, which was located near the center of Samaria and was the capital of the Kingdom of Israel.

Geographical Location

To the north, Samaria is bounded by the Esdraelon Valley, to the south, by the Jerusalem mountains. Samarian hills are not very high, seldom reaching over 800 meters. Samaria's climate is more hospitable than the climate further south.

Political Control

The History of Samaria in modern times begins in the aftermath of World War I, when the territory of Samaria, formerly belonging to the Ottoman Empire, is entrusted to the United Kingdom to administer as a British Mandate of Palestine, by the League of Nations. As a result of the 1948 Arab-Israeli War, the territory fell into the control of Jordan and residents would later receive Jordanian passports.

Samaria was taken by Israeli forces from Jordan during the 1967 Six-Day War. Jordan withdrew its claim to the West Bank, including Samaria, only in 1988, and later confirmed by Israeli-Jordanian peace treaty of 1993. Jordan instead recognized the Palestinian Authority as sovereign in the territory. In the 1994 Oslo accords, responsibility for the administration over some of the territory of Samaria was transferred to the Palestinian Authority.

Israel has been criticized for the policy of establishing settlements in Samaria. Israel's position is that the legal status of the land is unclear.

Samaritans

Ethnically, the Samaritans are the inhabitants of Samaria after the beginning of the Assyrian Exile of the Israelites. When Assyria overran the Northern Kingdom of Israel in 722 B.C.E., part of the population was deported, and other people from the Assyrian Empire were resettled in Israel. The new inhabitants worshipped their own gods, but when the then-sparsely populated areas became infested with dangerous wild beasts, they appealed to the king of Assyria for Israelite priests to instruct them on how to worship the "god of that country." The result was a syncretist religion, in which national groups worshipped the Lord, but also served their own gods in accordance with the customs of the nations from which they had been brought. Some Samaritans claim to be descendants of Israelites from the Northern Kingdom who escaped deportation and exile.

Samaritanism is a religion related to Judaism in that it accepts the Torah as its holy book, though little of later Jewish theology. The purported antagonism between Samaritans and Jews is important in understanding the New Testament stories of the "Good Samaritan" and the Samaritan woman.

History

Samaria was frequently besieged. In the days of Ahab, Benhadad II came up against thirty-two vassal kings, but was defeated with a great slaughter. A second time, the next year, he assailed it; but was again utterly routed, and was compelled to surrender to Ahab, whose army, as compared with that of Benhadad, was no more than "two little flocks of kids."

Samaria has been associated with John the Baptist, whose body was believed to be buried there. A small basilica church, first founded in the fifth century, was excavated on the southern slope of the acropolis. The church was believed to be the burial place of the head of John the Baptist. A monastery was added to it at a later date. In the twelfth century C.E., a Latin cathedral, also dedicated to John the Baptist, was built east of the Roman forum and combined elements of the Roman period city wall. It later became the Sebaste village mosque.

John 4:1-26 records Jesus' encounter at Jacob's well with the woman of Sychar, in which He declares Himself to be the Messiah.

The Samaritan Woman

Women of Samaria

The name "Samaria" derives from an ancient city of the same name, which was located near the center of Samaria and was the capital of the Kingdom of Israel. Samaria is one of the several standard statistical "areas" utilized by the Israel Central Bureau of Statistics. The history of Samaria in modern times begins when the territory of Samaria formerly belonging to the Ottoman Empire is entrusted to the United Kingdom to administer in the aftermath of World War I as a British Mandate of Palestine, by the League of Nations. As a result of the 1948 Arab-Israeli War, the territory fell into the control of Jordan and residents would later receive Jordanian passports.

Israel has been criticized for the policy of establishing settlements in Samria. Israel's position is that the legal status of the land is unclear.

Samaritans

The samaritans*Samaritans* are the inhabitants of Samaria, after the beginning of the Assyrian Exile of the Israelities*Israelites*, part of the population was deported and other peoples, were resettled in Israel. The new inhabitants worshiped their own gods, but when the populated areas became infested with dangerous wild beasts, they appealed to the King of Assyria for Israelite priests to instruct them on how to worship the "god of that country". The result was a religion in which national groups worship the Lord, but they also serve their own gods in accordance with the customs of the nations from which they have been brought. Some Samaritans claim to be descendants of Israelites from the Northern Kingdom who escaped deportation and exile.

Samaritan and the Jews are important in understanding the New Testament stories of "the Good Samaritan" and the Samaritan Woman.

The Samaritan Woman

Jesus left Judaea and again departed into Galilee. Being already in the north of Judaea, he chose the route which led through Samaria.

He left early in the morning to enjoy as many as possible of the cool hours for traveling. He stopped for rest and refreshment in the neighborhood of Sychar, a city not far from the well Jacob had bequeathed to his favorite son. The well, like many frequented wells in the east, was sheltered by a little alcove and there were seats of stone.

It was the hour of noon, and weary as He was with the long journey and the extreme heat, He sat on the well, and in His exhaustion flung his limbs wearily on the seat for complete repose. His disciples whom He had called among the earliest—probably the two pairs of brothers, and with them the friends of Phillip and Bartholomew—had left Him to buy in the neighboring city what was necessary for their wants. Hungry and thirsty, He sat wearily waiting for them, when His solitude as broken by the approach of a woman. The heat may indeed have been intense, but not too intense for moving about. This woman, either from accident or because she was in no good repute, would avoid the hour when the well would be thronged by all the women of the city coming to draw water. Water in the East was not only a necessity but a luxury.

Jesus would have hailed her approach, but He was thirsty and fatigued and had no means of reaching the cool water which glimmered deep below the well's mouth. He said to the woman "give me some water to drink."

Because of the hatred and rivalry between Jesus and the Samaritans, that request only elicited from the woman of Samaria an expression of surprise that it should have been made _____.

Gently the Lord tells her that had she known Him and asked of Him, He would have given living water. She pointed to the well, a hundred feet deep. He had nothing to draw with, so how could he obtain this living water? And then, perhaps with a smile of incredulity and national pride, she asked if He was greater than their father Jacob, who had dug and drunk of that very well? And yet there must have been something which struck her in His words, for now she addressed Him with the title of respect, which had been wanting in her initial address. She was thinking of common water for which he who drunk would thirst again; but the water He spoke of was a fountain within the heart, which quenched all thirst forever, and sprang up unto eternal life. She now became the suppliant.

He had asked her a little favor, which she had delayed; He now offers her an eternal gift. She sees that she is in some great presence, and begs for living water. She only begs for it that she might thirst no more, nor come there to draw.

Enough was done for the present to awake and instruct this woman. Jesus, abruptly breaking off this part of the conversation, bids her to call her husband

and return. All that was in His mind when He uttered this command we cannot tell. It was not positively wrong, for any man and above all for a Rabbi to hold a conversation with a strange woman. It may have been to break a stony heart, or awake a sleeping conscience. For she was forced to answer that she had no husband. She had had five husbands, and he whom she now had was not her husband.

She saw that a Prophet was before her, but on the facts of her own history she was naturally anxious to linger as little as possible. Her eager mind flew to the one great question, which daily agitated such fierce passion between her race and that of Him to whom she spoke, and which lay at the root of the savage animosity with which they treated each other.

Chance had thrown her into the society of a great Teacher: Was it not a good opportunity to settle forever the immense discussion between Jews and Samaritans. She put her dubious question: "Our fathers worshipped in their mountain and you say that Jerusalem is the place where men ought to worship."

He resolved her immediate problem. As against the Samaritans, the Jews were unquestionably right. Jerusalem was the place which God had chosen. He uttered to her the mighty and memorable prophecy that the hour was coming and now was, when "neither in this mountain nor yet in Jerusalem" should true worshippers worship the Father, but in every place should worship Him, in spirit and in truth.

She was deeply moved and touched. How could she at the mere chance word of an unknown stranger give up the strong faith in which she and her fathers had been born and bred? With a sigh she referred the final settlement of this and of every question to the advent of this Prophet, and then He spoke the simple words—"I that speak to you am He."

Words of immortal significance, to which all future ages would listen, had been uttered to this poor, sinful, ignorant stranger. Who would have imagined, who would have invented things so unlike the thoughts of man as these?

And here the conversation was interrupted, for the disciples return to their master. From a distance in that clear air they had seen and heard their master in a long and earnest conversation with a solitary figure. He a Jew, a Rabbi, talking to "a woman," and that woman a Samaritan, and that Samaritan a sinner! Yet they dared not suggest anything to Him nor question Him. Meanwhile the woman, forgetting even her water pot in her amazement, had returned to the city with her wondrous story. Here was one who had revealed to her the very secrets of her life, about the different men in her life, like Jesus saying to her go call your husband and come back, and the woman replied "I have no husband." "You are right to say you have no husband. The fact is you have had five husbands and the man you now have is not your husband. What you have said is quite true." The people of the town were so impacted with the woman's story that they came to see this Jesus. Even though this woman had a reputation as a loose woman, there was something about her transformation that made others believe. We want to so live our lives, that regardless of our past reputation, others will be able to see the transformation of our lives. God can use us as light in a dark world.

My Story

In August of 2004, I took a cruise to the Caribbean, I had a wonderful time. In each island we stopped we went on inner country trips, in which we learned a log about their culture, and how they make a living. On one of the tips we were taken in small boats to go to the main island to see how the residents do their shopping on a daily basis. On another one of our tip, we spent the day on the beach, the water was so blue and clean, even through it poured rain that day it did not stop us we partied in the rain. I would never forget that trip to the beach.

In the evening we would go back to the ships and relax for a while, then let go. Some of us went dancing, other went to the different shows, while other just wanted to sit around with their friends and have a quiet evening, but it was all worth the trip. After having such a wonderful time on that cruise, I decided to take another cruise the following year. I now have a passion for the learning the culture of other countries and other islands. These two trips encouraged me to write this book of my life story and how to live the life you love.

My name is Ismay Walker Harvey; I am the last child of seven siblings. I was born in Trinidad West Indies. My mom died when I was about eight years old. I grew up with my grandmother who raised my youngest brother and me. We never know our father, and the only memory I have of my mother is her selling candy in the elementary school I attuned and her coming to see my brother and I when she can. My second oldest brother also lived with us and was able to help the family financially, we were very poor. At the age of fourteen my grandmother became ill and I had to take care of her this was a difficult task for me seeing I was now in high school. I had to divide my time between my school work and taking care of my Grand Mother, she died when I was bout sixteen years old. After graduating from high school my older brothers and sisters helped out until I found employment, which was difficult. I migrated to the United States in October 1966. My first job was with the New York Telephone Company. I attended night school in which I receive my GED and some college credits, my other jobs were with Brooklyn Public Library, the Bank and finally with the city of New York, Department of Social Services as a Case-Worker where I worked for twenty five years 1976-2001 when I retired. The job was very interesting; I was able to help with the needs of single and family members. I enjoyed working with the public, especially with single mothers with young children. Because of my experience raising my son as a single mother, I was able to relate to their situations. The job also taught me what it was like to be on both sides of the fence. One year before working with the city of New York, I received Public Assistance/Welfare, but I was able to get my act together and by the Grace of God, I was able to get pass the New York City test, and was called for a position in the same building that I received Welfare, so I knew off hand what the clients were going through and how to communicate with them. It is so important to treat others the way we would like to be treated.

I am enjoying my retirement; I take trips out of the country about twice a year. One of my goals is to travel around the world since there is so much out there to see and learn. I would also like to get involved in world hunger and poverty and to contribute not only money, but my gifts, talents, and time helping others. I believe we are our brothers' keepers. My next goal is to be a good leader. Leadership is like beauty—hard to define, but you know it when you see it. Time has produced a legacy of outstanding and distinguished individuals who have impacted history and the development of mankind.

Our world needs direction, our communities need role models, our youth are begging for leaders they can look up to. They want to walk in their footsteps and not be ashamed or disappointed in their leadership. I believe with faith and perseverance I can make a difference in this world. Our world today is in desperate need of such individuals. My goal is to be in the team of individuals willing to take responsibility for the present situation and condition of the world, willing to face it head-on with integrity, character, and commitment. I was born and lived in a country that is considered a third-world country where people did not benefit from or participate in the industrial revolution. Even with this misconception, I believe that I have the ability to achieve, develop, accomplish, and fulfill the purpose I was created for, and in so doing I can one day say I have run the race and finished the course.

Being retired helps me to spend more time with my grandchildren, three girls, twelve, eleven, and five years old. I can take them to plays, on trips, and listen to them sing or watch them do the latest dances. They help keep me looking young and doing the things that I would otherwise not do. I love them, and my goal is to invest in their lives, and see them go to college, graduate, and be able to take care of themselves.

Other Women in the Bible

Eve—Adam's companion. No women after Eve got such an opportunity, after sin came into the picture.

Deborah—Judge and prophetess, she is one spectacular exception. She was a military leader, poet, prophet, and judge; she led a desperate nation to victory. Deborah was a mother and a wife; it is hard to think of an area in which Deborah did not excel. As a prophet, she had the ability to understand God's message and relay it to His people. She was also an accomplished poet.

Rachel and Leah—sisters who fought for years over Jacob. Rachel had the looks, as well as her husband's love. Jacob neglected Leah, whom he did not want to marry in the first place, but to make up for that, God gave Leah children, four sons. After a while, Jacob seemed to be just a fool in the struggle for dominance between two sisters.

Rebekah—Wife of Isaac, mother of Esau and Jacob. She was a forceful woman. She offered Abraham's servant to draw water for him and his camels, she not only went to the well she ran. Rebekah grabbed the chance of marriage to an unknown relative from hundred of miles away. Her family wanted time to adjust to the idea, but she got ready to leave the next day, never to see her home again. Rebekah waited twenty years to have a child and then gave birth to twins. God told her that Jacob, the younger, would be God's chosen. In an attempt to manage Jacob's success Rebekah pushed him into deceiving his father and stealing his brother's blessing. Rebekah thought she could control everything, regardless of whether her actions pleased God. The ploy worked as she predicted, but Rebekah had not foreseen the fury of Esau, Jacob's outwitted brother. Fearing for Jacob's life, she arranged to send him back to her childhood home. "When your brother is no longer angry . . . I'll send word for you to come back from there." For Rebekah that time never came. She died without seeing her favorite child.

Sarah—Abraham's wife, mother of Isaac. She was a beautiful woman, with a wonderful, healthy husband. Sarah should have been content, but her life revolved around one thing: the lack of having a child. Even though God had promised that her husband Abraham would father a great nation, the decades passed and Sarah remained childless. The odds of giving birth gradually dwindled. God's promise seemed laughable as Sarah celebrated her ninetieth birthday.

Sarah was a resourceful woman; she came up with an alternate plan. She would use her servant Hagar as a surrogate mother. Obviously feeling deep inner conflict about the decision, when Abraham got Hagar pregnant, Sarah mistreated her and sent her away. Hagar returned, but Sarah's inner conflict persisted. She drove mother and child into the desert. Meanwhile, God kept repeating the promise. Both Sarah and Abraham laughed at the notion. But the joke fell on them both, when Sarah finally got pregnant. After all her years of waiting, her longings were fulfilled. Sarah had a son, Isaac. Sarah was now in her nineties.

Hagar—Abraham and Sarah's Egyptian maidservant. She became a substitute wife for Sarah's husband. As was customary, a man could sleep with his servant and include her children in his household. Hagar slept with Abraham and she conceived. Knowing she was pregnant, she began to despise her mistress. Her pregnancy caused jealousy between the two women, and she was mistreated by her mistress, so she fled. Hagar then had an encounter with the Angel of the Lord, who told her to go back and submit to her mistress. Hagar obeyed and went back. She bore Abraham a son and named him Ishmael.

Miriam—Prophetess, sister of Aaron and Moses. At Moses' birth, Miriam was the hero, watching over her baby brother and cleverly jumping in to outwit Pharaoh's daughter. She took the spotlight again when the Israelites crossed the Red Sea, leading the women in a wild song of triumph. Miriam and her brother Aaron rejected Moses' wife, a foreigner. They were jealous and felt they ought to have equal spiritual status with Moses. "Has the Lord spoken only through Moses? Hasn't he also spoken through us?" God would not tolerate jealousy among the leaders of His people, especially jealousy aimed at the humble man whom He had chosen. He singled out Miriam, apparently the leader, for punishment.

Abigail—She had an instructive skill for diplomacy and peace-making. A woman of beauty and brains, she was not a main player in the history of Israel. She was married to Nabal, whom her parents chose for her. He was rich, which probably influenced Abigail's parents. Abigail knows her husband as a fool, and in one incident he was characteristically portrayed as being rude, drunk, and stupid.

Though being trapped in a bad marriage, she was hardly helpless. She took decisive action when her husband mistreated David, and she saved the day for her people as well as for David, who had lost his temper and was about to take vengeance that he would doubtless regret. He saw Abigail as a remarkable women and thanked her warmly, being a man of passions; he also had the courage to back down when challenged with good sense. Abigail, now being a widow, was asked by David to be his wife, and without hesitation she agreed. As a result of her wise decision she became linked to Israel's greatest king.

Elizabeth—Descendant of Aaron, wife of Zechariah the priest, and mother of John the Baptist. Elizabeth and her husband were advanced in age. She was barren, and their personal prayers to God were to have children. Elizabeth's husband, Zechariah the priest, had a visit from the Angel of God with good news; he was told that his wife Elizabeth would bear him a son, and he was to give his son the name John. Elizabeth became pregnant and remained in seclusion for five months. A short while later, a relative of Elizabeth named Mary, brought even greater news. The Messiah, the savior the Jews had been longing for, was on the way. Not only had God answered Elizabeth and her husband's personal prayers, their nation's long waiting would soon come to an end as well. Soon Elizabeth and her husband were bringing up the young and vigorous John the Baptist, a true original who would prepare the way for Jesus. They greeted the new era with joy; they saw the fulfillment of their dream.

Martha and Mary of Bethany—Martha and Mary lived in Bethany, a village outside Jerusalem. They had a close relationship with Jesus who loved them deeply, and had visited their home three or more times. Like many sisters, Mary was the type of person who could drop everything to listen to Jesus. When He called she answered. She showed her love for him in extravagant ways, lavishing a huge amount of expensive ointment on his feet (John 12:3). For her, everything stopped when Jesus was present. Mary's ways sometimes annoyed her sister Martha, who was obsessed about getting things done. Duty first was Martha's motto as she served Jesus by doing the housework and preparing meals. She preferred her own hard-working style, and asked Jesus to set Mary straight. "Martha, Martha," the Lord answered, "You are worried about and upset about many things, but only one thing is needed. Mary has chosen what is better, and it will not be taken away from her." (John 10:41, 42). In Bethany, at the home of Martha and Mary, after anointing Jesus with her expensive perfume, Mary was told by Jesus that her sins were forgiven. Your faith has saved you, go in peace. (Luke 7:36-50). Mary was healed from her sins much like the woman with the issue of blood that had a bleeding condition for twelve years and was healed by touching the hem or tassel of Jesus' cloak; she also was told that her faith had healed her, go in peace.

Mary the Mother of Jesus—Mary was chosen to mother God's son, which is the greatest honor; she was probably a teenager at the time. Mary had done nothing to deserve such favor. Her simple response spoke deeply of her humble faith. "I am the Lord's servant. May it be done to me as you have said." Mary said yes to God's plan to take over her life. She endured the doubts of Joseph and the scorn of neighbors who saw her pregnant before marriage. Saying yes meant bearing the pain of childbirth, and fleeing to far-off Egypt to protect her baby from Herod's soldiers. It meant raising a child she did not completely understand, but most of all it meant watching her son die on the cross. Our last glimpse of Mary shows her among the disciples after the resurrection praying for the Holy Spirit Jesus had promised. (Acts 1:14.) Mary had begun her relationship with Jesus by holding His tiny form in her arms. In the end, she realized she must let Jesus hold her. He was not only her child, He was her Lord. It all started with Mary's visit from the angel. She was a virgin at the time the angel said to her "Greetings, you are highly favored, the Lord is with you." Mary was greatly troubled by his words, and wondered what kind of greeting this might be. You will be with child, and give birth to a son, and you are to give him the name Jesus. "How will this be," Mary asked, "since I am a virgin?" The angel answered, "The Holy Spirit will come upon you and the power of the most high will overshadow you."

Mary Magdalene—Mary Magdalene is portrayed as a sensuous woman in movies and plays, sometimes as a reformed prostitute. In reality, the Bible gives no indication. It was known that she came from Magdala, a city on the Sea of Galilee. She was healed by Jesus and dedicated her life to him. Mary Magdalene headed the list of the women who helped finance his ministry.

Mary Magdalene stayed near Jesus and carefully observed where He was buried. After his crucifixion, she faithfully went there and cared for his body. She was the first person to see Jesus risen from the dead, and to spread the word. She told His disciples the news, and what He had said to her. (To be continued)

Hannah—Wife of Elkanah, was deeply loved by her husband, but she had an unfulfilled longing which made her life miserable. Hannah wanted a child. The longing for children may be the strongest in life. Today, infertile couples spend thousands of dollars in search of a medical remedy. Hannah was blessed by God but her longing outweighed every blessing. Hannah wept, felt bitter, and poured out her heart to God. Hannah had a rival. Elkanah would give portions of the meat to his wife Peninnah and her children, but to Hannah he gave a double portion because he loved her, and the Lord had closed her womb. (1 Samuel 1:1-6 NIV.) Hannah kept praying to God. "O Lord Almighty, if you would only look upon your servant's misery and remember me, and give me a son, I would give him to the Lord for all the days of his life."

God answered Hannah's prayer and gave her a son, Samuel. She poured out the joy to God. She took Samuel to God's tabernacle as soon as he reached an appropriate age.

Hannah loved her child and never forgot him. She did not cling to her blessing any more than she clung to her woes. She gave both to God.

Jezebel—The proud, determined daughter of a king, she came from Sidon on the Mediterranean coast, where her father reigned. She was married to Ahab, King of Israel. Jezebel had set out single-handedly to force Israel into paganism and nearly on her husband Ahab, who sold himself to do evil in the eyes of the Lord. Only one man dared to oppose her publicly: the prophet Elijah. Yet even his amazing triumph failed to vex her, it only made her worse; she wanted to kill Elijah, not convert him.

Jezebel died as she lived; when her luck ran out, she did not beg for mercy. She dressed up for the showdown, and waited at the window for the man who had to deal with her. She was tossed out the window by her own servants, and the town dogs devoured her body. When they went out to bury her, they found nothing except her skull, her fell, and her hands.

Esther—Esther was a hero who was in the right place at the right time. True heroes recognize the crisis, and move to meet it. This kind of courage made Esther great. Queen Esther was a Jew. King Xerxes was looking for a beautiful young lady to be his bride. His personal attendant decided to make a search for beautiful young virgins for the King. These virgins were placed under the care of Hegel, the King's eunuch, who would be in charge of the women and their beauty treatments and let the girl who pleased the King be queen instead of Vashti. Esther, who was also known by the name Hadassah, was raised by her cousin Mordecai; she had neither father nor mother. Esther was lovely in form and features, and Mordecai had taken her as his own daughter after the death of her parents. Esther also was taken to the King's palace, and entrusted to Hegel. The girl pleased the King and won his favor. He assigned to her seven maids, selected from the King's palace. Mordecai had forbidden Esther to reveal her nationality and family background. Mordecai had high connections in the palace, and was able to keep an eye on Esther and how she was doing and what was happening.

Esther completed twelve months of beauty treatments before her turn came to go to King Xerxes. Anything she needed was given to her to take with her from the harem to the King's Palace. When Esther's turn came to go into the palace, she asked for nothing. Esther won the favor of everyone who saw her. She was taken to King Xerxes, who was more attracted to Esther than to any of the other women. Esther won his favor and approval, so he set a royal crown on her head, and made her queen instead of Vashti. He gave a great banquet for all his nobles and officials (Esther's banquet) and proclaimed a holiday, distributing gifts throughout the province.

Queen Esther's story was part of God's plan to save the Jews. She alone, of all the Jews, had access to the king. A vengeful and evil prime minister named Haman made up his mind to destroy the Jews. Queen Esther's cousin Mordecai reminded her of her unique place, and that she had come to a royal position for such a time as this. This is the end?